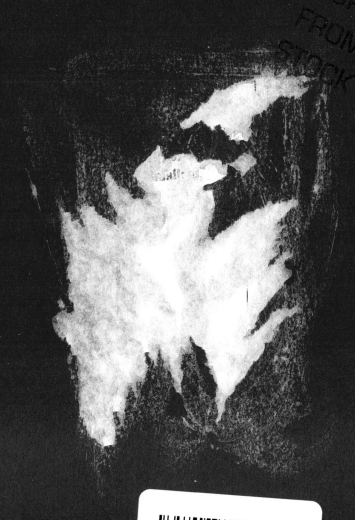

D1351386

Gallery Books
Editor Peter Fallon

MIDNIGHTSTOWN

Tom French

MIDNIGHTSTOWN

Gallery Books

Midnightstown
is first published
simultaneously in paperback
and in a clothbound edition
on 28 May 2014.

The Gallery Press
Loughcrew
Oldcastle
County Meath
Ireland

www.gallerypress.com

© Tom French 2014

ISBN 978 1 85235 601 9 *paperback*
    978 1 85235 602 6 *clothbound*

A CIP catalogue record for this book
is available from the British Library.

Contents

*to the memory
of Anne Kennedy*

The Delivery Room

James Henry French, b. 20.11.2003

They had wheeled your mother to theatre
in a plunge-back gown for the performance
of a lifetime, and left us to keep company
at her bedside after the bed was gone —

you on the flat of your back in an incubator,
a spaceman, minutes old, taking it all in
and taking your time about sampling the air.
Someone is going to tell you, so let it be me —

because the blood and the heat were too much
I lifted the sash window and, slipping my head out
for a breath of air, took in the cemetery — the skip
parked inside the gate for withered wreaths,

the far corner, filled with innocents, still green,
row upon row of neat marble and granite,
the only sound a car on the Bridge of Peace
and an ambulance idling at A&E.

We will never be in a room as full or as empty.
The first voices we heard were voices off —
night sisters whispering, nearing their shift's end,
that the night just gone had felt like an eternity.

Flock

for Andrew Bennett

All this week, between us
and the sea, starlings
in their thousands have been

flocking, darkening
the sky in the hour before
the sky itself darkens.

Three floors up, above
the stage of The Peacock,
weeks before you get

to grips with lines and text,
in a rehearsal room
the furniture's pushed back

and a cast is taking
time out of its life to flock,
all banking and turning

when one banks and turns,
mimicing birds to make a play
because the smoothness

of their flocking depends on trust.
An hour south of us
daylight, like house lights, dips.

Starlings on the roofs
of The Plough and The Tide
are startled by a flash of faces,

a phalanx of backs,
as a downdraught happens
and the curtain lifts.

A Roll Call

i.m. Peggie Kerbey (1923-2012)

A whole half-century before you told
your grandchild she'd been out before
and she said, 'I was, Peg. And I'm going
out again', we find ourselves searching
on the morning of your last day on Earth
for you in the rolls of Kentstown Girls'
National School, and find you at last
close to the door on the morning of your first day,
hiding behind your maiden name in Irish
in the old *cló* beside the *X* that makes you
present and correct, the wise child taking
things in, being taken in by nothing,
who was out before, and is going out again.

Fires

1

My mother told me how the church was saved
by someone in the small hours spotting smoke.
She said that marble cracked, organ pipes glowed
white hot and belched like chimney stacks,
stone fonts ran bone-dry. She went into the dark

weeks after — steeplejacks abseiling like saints
in the air above the altar, cleaning the ceiling
with *J Cloths* and squeegies to stem the soot-rain —
into the pains they took to lift the dirt and leave
the mural's beautifully executed wounds untouched.

I believed she was speaking the antiphon to me —
'This is my son, my belovèd, in whom is my delight' —
as we wished each other peace and stepped into the light,
and the great rose window blossomed into flame.

2

All those nights we slept, he fought the blaze.
Out every road, for days, summer fires burned.
Now it's dawn. He smoulders in the yard,
cupping a *Gold Bond*, bearing our shovel,
his bull's wool tunic drapes from a shoulder.

I've come to the back kitchen door to see
what the weather is doing on The Devil's Bit,
and close it again against turf smoke, burnt furze,
my father, turning his black face towards me
as if to speak, bent double, returned, beyond words.

Prayer

after the Irish of Séamus Dall Mac Cuarta

I am too long sprawled abroad in Louth,
brought by torment to the end of strength.
Rouse yourselves now. Assemble the men
to shoulder my bones to the bone orchard.

Legion were the courts and the strongholds
where I held my own and saw the dawn.
Would silence have garnered more favour,
O God of Grace, and sped me to Heaven?

I gave my life's days composing songs
instead of repenting as I should've done.
But now that I am sick and up against it,
Christ Jesus, have mercy on Séamus Dall.

An Amelanchier in Ministown

Putting our weight to the stake supporting
the tree you planted for your mother
that flowers in the month of her death

we feel her hand on our forearms again,
steadying herself, steadying us, bending
as it strengthens, strengthening as it bends.

Audite Omnes

The fair at Dunshaughlin was in full swing
as Seachnall wrestled with his '*Audite Omnes*',
so he sent word to keep it down or knock it off
because the racket was hampering composition.

But the message went unheeded, so Seachnall —
raising his hands to Heaven — upped the ante,
whereupon thirteen chariots were swallowed whole
and the rest perished in the lake of Lagore.

Lake current reined in mares, colts, stallions,
flesh strained at the bit against clay for air
and bridles and bellybands were turned to flotsam;

then Seachnall settled, took the goose pen again
in his trembling hand, and beautiful verses
occurred to him in that silence of drowned horses.

Scarecrows

Your class is planting cress
and mustard seeds in single pots
on the warm sill, writing out

the phrase *We will watch them
grow*, and cutting out
outfits for the scarecrows,

one for everyone in the room.
Maedhbh and Eve have brought
hay from home for under the hats.

There's even a song! What hope
of mustard or cress have the birds
when a scarecrow guards every seed?

General Tom Thumb Takes the Pledge

Tom Thumb's visit to Europe coincided with the onset of the Great Hunger. In February 1847 . . . the ship taking him back to the US passed the Irish coastline . . .
— Christine Kinealy, *History Ireland,*
January/February 2014

Before you forsake your thimbleful
of Negus for the sake of your soul, raise,
Tom, a penultimate (since the bird never
flew on one wing) thimble to the thousands

who line the quay as you take leave, to steal
a glimpse of your symmetrical proportions
receding on the poop deck toward the horizon
where a New World awaits, in unreserved seats,

your shilling histories and turns as a Hercules
who's taken the weight of a shrunken world
to heart, matched the mermaids round for round,

and drunk the Siamese twins under the table.
The Large Room is empty. Starvation is come.
We shall not look upon your likes again.

Southern Star / Realt a' Deiscirt

*A middle-aged, reliable horse, quiet and kind to all work. Apply
James French, Ballyroe, Leap.*
— *The Southern Star*, 13 March 1948

Between a V8 with hackney plates (Toormore),
a capable girl to take charge of a bar, pocket combs,
bottle *Brilliantine*, a mare in foal to *Sunshine* at Rahine,
ricks of oaten straw, freehold shops, fine swagger coats,

back-to-back traps, broody hens from Inchafume,
a *Pohlman* piano (steel frame, pristine),
they have led one another to the end of the lane.
Among cycling suits (satisfaction asssured), turkey hens,

('fine gander — what offers?'), a *Melotte* Separator
in perfect working order, *Arran Banners* grown
from Athlone seed, *Aylesbury* duck eggs
from Lisheencreagh, guinea eggs (Lissangle),
my father's father is hanging up his tackle.

Between a cart with foundry axle (Coolanuller),
a *Baby Ford* (Lissarda) in sterling condition,
shallots (sound to eat), a *Singer* foot machine,
Abundance seed oats from Ahaliskey,
this man and his mare are parting company.

Among *Ellam's Early, Flower of Spring,
Daniel's Defiance*, Lisbelad mangolds, a timber cot,
Hornsby corn drill (must be seen), violin (no bow,
with case), from Laravoulta a Shorthorn roan,
this horse, her *Chevalier*, are going their own roads.

Among winnowing machines (complete with screens),
reasonable pups by *Musical Hammer, Imperial* churn
(Miss Good, Currycrowley), nice sows (first litter),

Aughadown, a dozen cocks from Coornishal,
this man and his work horse are throwing in the towel.

Among chestnut fillies from Keelovenogue,
bran bags, brass caps, tackling (Cloughgriffin),
sows due to farrow in the last days of spring,
half sacks, bedsteads, chains, ploughs, parts,

a promising draught (Keelnacronaugh, trial given),
ryegrass by the bushel from Coppeen,
a zig-zag harrow all the way from Shanaway,
my father's father is surrendering his reins.

Among acres of stubble and acres of grazing,
Ailsa Craigs and *Woodward's Open Airs*,
a cob (not wanted) in Crohane,
Khaki Campbell duck eggs (Department strain),
the finest first crop hay from Skeaf,
they have broken their last sweat together in these fields.

Between springing heifers, leather clippings,
Spiller stoves, works by Dickens,
beet pulp, lathe & bench (complete),
'other works by Wodehouse and Annie Smithson',
this mare goes on from here without her man.

Among springer pups from Knockanuss,
scufflers (lovely, Kilbrogan Cross),
grindstone and anvil from Cullinane,
Wyandotte hatchlings from Derryduff,
this horse and her master have had enough.

Among cows due to calve in Curraghlickey,
chrysanthemum stools from Clonakilty,
a certain cure for ringworm from Boulteen,

clover, vetches, Italian grasses,
a car (with boards) from Droumadava,
this steed and this trojan are going no farther.

A Relic

It gave no cure. Its only gift was peace.
I drove with it, printed linen sealed in aluminium,
in its flight case on the passenger seat,
oil from the Holy Land, a prayer on a card to recite.

'"Mary" is her name, isn't it? "Mary"?' the saintly
woman who lent those things asked over the phone,
which shut me up, since she had no way of knowing.
That turned out to be her last night in that house.

How she made it upstairs to bed I don't know.
In the small hours I woke to her 'Tom . . . I have to go.'
So I rose to hunt the linen from under her duvet,
warm still with the last of her heat. And we went.

Page 9, Irish Independent, 17 February 1987

Years later I zoom out to read the names
of all the other people who died that day,
'peacefully', *'beloved'*, *'deeply regretted'*
by grandchildren and great-grandchildren, mostly;

'unexpectedly' where somebody harboured
hopes of a recovery; only one other *'suddenly,*
following an accident', which makes the grief
'inexpressible', the parents *'heartbroken'*.

Our codes for grief rub shoulders with pairs
of antique beds, ham slicers, kitchen scales;
someone with the initials *'GB'*,
in return for a favour granted, publishes his thanks;

and, at the foot, the meteorological situation —
a northeast airflow covering the country,
snow showers near the coast, frost at first,
sunny spells, an outlook for little change —

3°C and cloudy in Amsterdam
where they shipped his body from,
and 3°C in Dublin too. Had he passed
through the Arrivals Hall's glass doors

and launched, without pausing for breath,
into all that had befallen since we'd met
we might've marked the rain he'd left behind.
We might've told him to his face he'd brought the sun.

A Night

1 DOONA, SUNSET

for Bob Brennan

Because nobody comes between us and the sun
we will be silhouettes forever on Doona Strand.

2 CARRIGILLIHY, DAWN

for Mary O'Driscoll

Like someone in the room breathing with me,
the sea, returning over the gravel, to the sea.

A Limousine in Carrigillihy

For twenty summers in his hearse
parked on Mary O'Driscoll's grass that gives
onto treacherous rocks named
'The Treacherous Rocks', a pair of islands
going by 'Adam' and 'Eve' where the cattle
are herded by the sea, that you can see
from Mary's south-facing settee,
Charlie Shearer slept the sleep of the dead.

He sleeps upstairs like one of the family now
while his paintings of the house he sleeps in
hang downstairs. In a corner of the garden
in one, under flowering buddleia, is the car,
the driver's window lowered to let in air,
where Charlie has painted himself asleep,
dreaming of painting where a corpse would be.

Midnightstown

In exchange for the gift of a cherry tree
I drop next door a bootleg of *Chants Juifs.*

*

Striking out west from the back door,
we are stopped, as by the sea, by a ploughed field.

*

Trying not to fall, I find myself whistling the air
of track four — 'The Tight-rope Walker's Prayer'.

*

Overnight our one big tree came to ground;
we went the night without hearing a sound.

*

Stormy for days; next door's collie's hoarse
from letting the east wind know who's boss.

*

Who is the man who waves as if he knows us
when it's only the dog he walks we recognize?

*

April 4th, our cherry looks to be in full bloom;
I hear 'The Kaddish' issue faintly from their sun room.

A Jug of Contrast

Here it is everyone's birthday.
The nurse brings jugs of contrast
to rest on tables in the waiting area.
Everyone gets a full one to himself.

Behind the door gifts are being given.
She hands out party bags as we leave,
with images inside of our insides —
no bones, just the soft tissue gleaming.

The Verge of Tears

an oncology diary

The names of the wards start with a big *C* —
Cedar, Catherine, Cara, Cherry —
this is a strategy to deal with fear,
at the main door, letter by letter.

*

I drink the tea she doesn't feel up to
and look away while they search for a vein.
(Because they soak her hands sometimes

to make it easier, all it takes is morning,
my children's breakfast bowls steeping
in the sink, to bring her hands to mind.)

*

On the site for the new hospital
a crane driver has planted his county flag
on the boom of his crane. When they raised it

in the depths of winter he must've been
imagining the end of summer,
the city ablaze with his county colours.

*

Hundreds of channels and still we wind up
watching a miniature John Deere
on the fairway of the course next door,
mowing the first growth this year

in a snow flurry that thickens to a blizzard.
How have I lived more than four decades
and not seen grass being cut in snow?

*

When was the last time I noticed her scapular bones?
They have never been so clear. At the deepest point
of the *V* in the oncology nurse's scrubs
I can't help glimpsing and thinking *'aureolae'* —
a charm as good as the next against death.

*

We go halves on the giant biscuit
that has reached its *Best Before*,
before I give in and take the lion's share.

Her desire to feed me is stronger than ever —
sandwiches for later, fruit in danger of going off,
a dollop of mayonnaise in a night light holder.

*

I am trying to make out the crane driver's face
through two panes of glass, a sealed vacuum
filled with colourless gas, a sheet of tinted perspex
through which two tubes enter,
as though the room itself were on oxygen.

'Jesus, don't take her now. Not while
the children are still small. Give her
a few years free of the misery' —
I pray to the man in the crane.

*

When we slip out for an early bird
she pulls her sleeve discreetly down
to conceal the wristlet that bears her name
and DOB, which leaves me
picturing her in her first weeks.

*

To the legendary TV memory man
who passes while we eat and smiles,
she tells me after, she was on
the verge of saying, 'You that has
the great memory, do you remember me?'

*

There — floodlit in the dark —
is the enormous cedar
which gives the ward its name.
How could a body not take heart

from the sight of the limb it lost
last winter and survived, the pale flesh
under the bark, the wound still fresh?

*

There has been so much talk of odds
and chances, we could be leaving
a casino, with our purses lightened,
moving toward the car in *Set Down Only*.

The shadow of the crane boom
passes over. A weight leaves the earth,
heavenward. No one catches anyone's eye.
No one is getting away with his life.

02.07.2012

It is impossible that the child of so many tears should be lost.
— St Ambrose

*None of us got it his own way . . . It seemed better that we
kept alive.*
— W D Snodgrass, *'Heart's Needle'*

All of our options are exhausted.
It is like God leaving the room
when the oncologist takes his leave.
A man of the cloth comes with oils
and we say your name over and over, 'Hail Mary . . .'

*

Out behind the corpse house
in the shade of the evergreens,
the undertaker's son, relaxing

in the passenger seat, sizes up
a woman on Page 3. I came
seeking directions from him
and leave, envying her her health.

*

What his father says is good enough
almost to engrave on a headstone —
'If we lose each other on the Canal
we'll meet up again at The Poitin Still.'

*

On your second last day you send us
across the street from the hospital

to learn again what it means to eat.
Italy were playing Spain at sunset.

Potato and asparagus soup to start,
then beautiful lamb stew,
a list of pizzas as long as your arm.
The owner at the window table, taking time

out to dine before the rush, accepted
patrons' wishes for the Azzurri,
a citizen cherishing a half glass of wine,
his silhouette, a picture of how to live.

＊

The last time you used the words 'I am' —
'You'd better talk, because I'm not able.'

＊

In Thurles a couple pushing a buggy,
a man on his knees, lost in the sacrament
of trimming his front hedge and sweeping
the trimmings with his kitchen brush,
stopped to cross themselves.

Motorists switched off their engines
in the street and went on about
their errands only after the inevitable,
polished so they could see themselves in it,

had passed.

＊

'Is Maureen home? Tell her
not to come. I don't want her
to see me like this.'

*

There is time for the sister who brought
sustenance on a tray for the months
when you sat upstairs in the room with Grief,
not speaking, with the curtains pulled, to say,
'Mary, I brought you something small. Eat.'

*

Searching for ways to be kind
we offer ice, water from a straw.
John brushes your hair. I recall
your father in his Sunday clothes,

milking by hand, the white arc
of warm milk in the byre dark
entering our mouths, across the yard
from the house you were born in.

*

After the central line goes in
there's nothing they don't know.
We watch your heart on the screen
like a beacon.

*

I hear John saying what he said
again and again to gain admission

at the intercom to *High Dependency* —
'We are Mary French's sons.'

*

'Mary, your sons are here . . .'
'They're always here . . .'

*

They are slipping my mind,
the handful of times you said *'Thurles'*
as a single syllable, to rhyme with *'Arles'*,

where a crying child, where you grew up,
was told her crying would be heard.

*

I want what you said when I offered you
my arm in case you fell to be remembered —

'If I fall, you can come back for me.
But I am not holding on to anyone.'

*

You would be thinking
of us in transit today.

Who do we ring to say
that the roads were quiet,
that we got there safe?

*

On a morphine pump nestled
between pillows, bearing beads
of moisture on its breath —
this is how kindness leaves the earth.

Saturday 31 June-Monday 2 July 2012

Late Encounters

1 AT KNOCKNACARRA CHURCH

He was the perfectly balanced Irishman
in the end — the glycerine spray in one
anorak pocket, ten *Gold Bond* in the other,
hailing myself and my two-year-old son

with, 'You've a great little walker there',
then falling silent as we drew near
and it dawned on him that there was blood
between the two of us, and the two of them.

2 A LAMINATED HURLEY

His hurley fallen asunder in his hands,
I come upon him, like the child in the tale
on a mission, bearing the thing that will change
everything if he can arrive in time

and thwart fate, gathering *cippins* on his hands
and knees in the six yard box of the pitch
they took the hill from, and I am tempted
to kneel and help him.

Because it had no grain it had no spring,
and there was no one tree its timber came from.
To *French* through *de Freyne* from *Fraxinus*,
my father's name comes down to me from *ash*.

In Memory

I IN FUREY'S

We couldn't drink to the things that spring
to mind — the future, the next generation,
good health. Too sick from chemotherapy
to face homemade lasagne and thick-cut chips,

you ordered us brandy, the decent stuff.
Close to the stove, in the back, we drank
to our loved and unloved, living and dead,
to the rest of the road home, the night ahead.

2 ABBEYLEIX, 6 JULY 2012

Today is your birthday. It has rained all day.
We make ourselves at home in the children's library
where we try to remember the colour of your eyes
and can't believe you won't open them again.

The children are playing Close Your Eyes and See
What God Sends You. Someone raises a window
for air, and we breathe in the Sensory Gardens.
We close our eyes, and the thought of hazel comes.

3 BULBS

The atrium is filled with us, the bereaved
of the last year, gathered together,
waiting for the wax in the candles to set
before we can take them away, our faces
still warm from their heat, and go back
to our lives with crocus bulbs in our pockets
like change, to plant when we get home.

4 STRAW

In the first days I did a thing
I'd never done, reached into
her purse and felt miraculous
medals among coins, a laminated
prayer, legal tender, driver's license,
a shopping list, straw from the crib,
the charm against an empty purse.

5 MONTH'S MIND

We found where the withered flowers go.
Now that you know your way around
you come in a dream, doing what you used to,
healthy again and on the verge of laughing.

I take your forearms in my palms, grateful
that you came and say, 'Mam, you're supposed
to be dead', and you go, barely able
to contain yourself, 'I know. I know.'

Edward McGuire's Portraits

1 'ANTHONY CRONIN'

This is a 'Grace Before Meals' where even
the pattern on the dinner plate gives thanks
and the tidy iron pot is filled to the brim
with a succulent casserole, or licked clean.

All that remains to iron is the tablecloth.
He sustains his own head in his two hands.
We are given this trellis to help take in the sky.

2 'PEARSE HUTCHINSON'

The body by the soul cannot be kissed
without one voluptuous lip, at least.

3 'S B SMITH'

In the absence of birthmark, face, fingerprints,
by the pattern of purl and plain stitches
in his crew-necked jumper, he will be known
to the one who listens for his hand on the latch.

4 'EAMON MORRISSEY'

The grain of the wood in a kitchen chair,
its struts and uprights and dovetail joints;

the sitter's wrists crossed as if to accommodate
the nail that enters and leaves by his watch face.

My Father Flying

My father is teaching himself
to fly in our bathroom mirror.
I spy on him from the cubby hole
where our coats and holy water are.

He sticks newspaper to shaving cuts
to stem the flow, then starts to touch
the tips of his fingers together
behind his back, then swings

his arms above his head where
fingertips meet again, counting
as he does this, breathing out
on the downbeat, then wipes

the mirror clear, washes five o'clock
shadow from the sink and goes
about his business. The time
is coming when I must do this too —

stand, morning after morning, before glass
while my son spies on me,
proving, as I walk into the day, to him,
that the air is not our realm.

The Bridge of Peace

Set cement, a scrap of soil;
an ash seed germinates in a *Nike* sole.
It still won't come, nor go away,
the other name the people
of Connemara had for Bruce Ismay.

I kept what my father said
in his last year, as he looked me
in the eyes, in my head —
'All the people I love are dead.'

Crows finish a chow mein and cross
when the green man permits. Say
'We are taking water', never 'We're sinking'.
It dawns as the lights turn. *Brú Síos Mé.*

In the Mirror

1 CHICK'S, DOMINICK STREET

He has run his cut-throat over the jugulars of our fathers
so, if Chick's door is open and no one is there,
feel free to slip in off the street and contemplate,
in the absence of Chick, the tools of Chick's trade —

boar hair brushes, pomades and strop, that photograph
of JFK in an open-top limousine, one hand aloft,
taken from the far side of the street to take in the shop,
and eavesdrop, through the beauty board, to the shop

next door where Chick has popped to throw an eye
over the field, to have a flutter and coax a long shot
home before he slips back to his dapper reflection
to minister and not pass judgement on the heads
whose contours he has known better than his own.

2 THERMOPYLAE

Of all the orders passed down hours before
the strangest was the one to tend their hair,
but being Greek they set side-arms aside,
unbuckled body armour and picked up combs.

Then perfumed oils and salves and costly lotions
passed, by camp light, among those remaining
with instructions from their bloodiest, Leonidas,
to comb each other's heads and tend their manes

and, after they'd rendered each other this service,
to gather the stray ends together in a simple tail
to hang free of the neck and leave the eyes clear
to see the beautiful death they prayed to Eros for.

3 A TRIM

He extends to me, as he did to my sisters,
the two uneven Os of our household scissors
in the hopes that I might bring myself to trim
the strands at the back that prove beyond him.

He has knelt up and promised to be good.
If he stirs a muscle now there will be blood.
Thus we grow accustomed to addressing each other —
I, to his temple; he, to my face in the mirror.

Since we have said all there is to say of weather —
It broke. It held. It broke. It held. It broke, father —
and this is his last visit and he is going away,

and I have drawn the line at eyebrows and nostrils,
I present him with an eyebrow pencil with which
he makes the *F* upright, its high rungs, the '*rench*'.

4 TED LEAN'S GENTS HAIRDRESSING

In Ted Lean's in Thurles you had to kneel up,
then Ted leaned in with buzz shears and comb
to neaten the sides and take a bit off the top.
He raised you with his foot pump invisibly

till you were eye-level with breakables arrayed
on plate glass, *4711*, cut-throats disinfecting
in blue fluid, magnified. The letters of 'L E A N'
arching on the pane like a saloon's, and the comb

with a built-in bubble to level heads were last things
before the glass raised; then the shock of cold air

46

coming off the Suir as you stepped, brushed down
and perishing, into Liberty Square.

Messines

One man dons a stethoscope to eavesdrop,
through earth, for a breaking of wind, a cough.

Tunnelling through chalk without making a sound
makes the men, not stone deaf, but snow blind.

The cure is a trip up the incline
to take in the sky.

*

Because all of their uniforms are white
and no one can see, when two snow-blind parties meet

they trace the contours of each other's faces
with chalky fingertips to determine friends, enemies.

*

They would pass for performance artists —
the one who operates the spade with his feet,

the second who stops dug chalk from falling,
the last who bears the spoil to the light.

As house lights gutter out for want of air
each matinée brings them closer to the night.

*

To the names of the ones who will never be found
add the canary whose last breath is all his keepers
lived for, whose posthumous decorations for bravery
will be its wing- and tail- and chest-feathers.

*

It brings us
closer to peace,
imagining

a skylark
waiting
for silence to sing.

Fred Bennett's Cigarettes

With best wishes for a Happy Christmas and a Victorious New Year,
from The Princess Mary and Friends at Home

A lifetime since your lungs were decommissioned
your tobacco issue comes under the hammer —
foil wrapped for freshness, and turning to dust.
Bidders, like the shell-shocked, touch
extremities as if to check they are still there —
the tip of a nose, the lobe of an ear, a fontanelle.
One waves an auction catalogue in surrender
as you elevate a Lucifer to the tip, and inhale.

Tans

Not one who was there forgets, nor speaks thereafter
of the four who entered, crossed the flags for water
and left without a word, of the mugs they drank from
borne outside and beaten with a hammer into powder.

Reading to My Father

Once, and only once, I read to him
in a car pulled over on the hard shoulder
on the Mountrath road, a stone's throw
from The Wishing Tree, every word

of my brother's diary, his suicide note,
the phrases in Dutch that meant 'I will
soon be dead', those marginal doodles,
little Golgothas, tiny crosses on stones.

While he smoked and couldn't not hear,
locked in the car, I read to that last page
because this would be our last time together.

Neither of us knew what would happen next.
A son reads to his father. The world ends.
The son is driving. They are going nowhere.

An Outfit

. . . so that the threads I have spun may not be altogether wasted.
— *The Odyssey*, Book 19

I will find it suits me
               down to the ground
when I finish weaving
               my father's shroud.

Artaud on Aran

If travelling light in the upper storeys
in the Free State in the '30s had been a crime
the arrests would've had to have started early
and gone on for an indecent length of time.

You weren't the first to resort to the society
of sea and stone, to wind up where *peyote*
and *poitín* meet at the periphery of the mind,
and find the North Atlantic *un peu de trop*.

Your offences — finding the bare necessities
beyond your means, and not being from here.
The campaign to restore us to ourselves ends

with a one-way drive in an unmarked car
through the sleeping capital to its quays,
and a plainclothes' *Adieu* falling on deaf ears.

Intermission (Blues)

1 PIAF

They were too in fright, the night
The Little Sparrow died,
of the dress she sang in all her life
to hang it on its hanger right.

When it hit the wardrobe floor
the wardrobe hinges creaked
the first four notes of *La Vie en Rose*.

2 SAINT JOHN COLTRANE

He slipped out in the intermission
with binoculars
to gaze at the stars for inspiration.

When he returns he'll wet and slip,
as the night wind wets the reeds,
the reed between his lips.

3 MOONSHINE

Guitar strings and spirits were all the one;
Blind Lemon Jefferson knew by listening

to the jug how his whiskey was lessening.
He filled that thrashed guitar up to the brim.

Ballyroe, 20 February 1930

Hannah, the grandmother I never met,
tiptoes across the floor
of *Births, Deaths & Marriages*
to peer over my shoulder

as I date and sign a cheque
to pay for my father's birth cert
and try again to believe her eyes
as she listens for his breath.

The Five Trees, October 19th

The last few red leaves on one are still hanging on.
The trees will be ready for winter when they're gone.

An Airman in Mornington

1

You could have knocked the longshoremen
of Mornington over with a feather that dawn
at the tail end of the war when they hauled
you up with their long-handled mussel rakes
from their ancestral mussel beds off Mosney
for a last shore leave destined to last Eternity.

2

Cap and cap badge and insignia were at sea,
so it fell to them to frisk you where you lay
among the first catch bound for an early train,
for what you pocketed when you left your bed
for the air — a last will and testament, *'mother'*,
'leave', *'possess'* in waterproof pencil, dog tags,
marks, a comb to keep the fringe from your eyes.

3

Because yours is the only entry in the *Register
of Interments of Bodies of Persons Washed Ashore*
this has the air of an abandoned book

in which the sexton, a fisherman moonlighting
among gravestones with shovel and pick,
had the presence of mind to sketch a freehand map —

a square, a line, an *X* within earshot of bird calls
that fall on deaf ears where you touched down,
to shake out, like a vestment, your parachute to air.

O'Casey, Hurling

How far from 20/20
can his vision have been
to take a bird in flight
for a fifty-fifty cross,

to connect with it in mid-
air, and send that ball
of blood and bone and feather
soaring over the bar?

Oileán Thoraí

after Pat Collins

Let us waken slowly to the wardrobe
slipping its moorings, to the buoy music
wire hangers make, to belongings, hand-me-downs
setting sail, to Holy Marys, periwinkles, shells
making themselves at home on our bedroom floor
among hair strands, dust balls, shed skin,

and accept from the hands of our one neighbour
who crosses from the mainland in a light craft
fashioned from sallies and the skin of a single cow
the leaves that he claims grow there in abundance,
that he passes out on the quay like tender.

The Middle Reaches

for Tony Holten

It's taken half my lifetime to come
                              eye to eye with an otter.
It'll take the next half to forget
                         how we regarded one another.

An Outfit

Choosing an outfit
    for your earthly remains
we throw open your wardrobe,
    and your scent escapes.

          *

Though your body is going
    nowhere forever,
we find ourselves
    thinking of your feet,
        considering footwear,
the occasion you're dressing for,
          the weather.

          *

Buttoned cuffs to cover
    the embalmer's wound,
a string of fake pearls,
    that purple wool jacket,
        a white blouse, soft collar,
          open at the throat.

          *

The garments assembled,
    we stand back to look
        at them on their hanger,
    how they go together,
      the way
    that you might look
          at yourself in a mirror.

To Tommy Murray in Heaven

The first dustings of snow fell across some of the more high-lying regions of the country yesterday . . . Over the next few days it's going to be on the cold side of normal.
              — Met Éireann, Friday, 2 November 2012

It is as if you have held your breath to hear
the first light snow of winter fall on the hills,
into the freshets from the stony uplands
on Newtown, Camp David and Shanlothe,
Castel Gandolfo, Tullyglass and Balmoral,
between the last church pew and the porch,
the mass paths and the mixed marriages,
on the lemmings, kingfishers and crows,
the outcast, the yeti, on the mislaid rosary
and 'the marsupially challenged kangaroo',
the wheelbarrow, wagtails and guillemots,
into the saucepan left to prime an iron pump,
to become, when it falls into the half-barrel
in the forge in your mind, forge water, a cure.

'Visiting Samuel Menashe'

i.m. Samuel Menashe (1925-2011)

The bathtub may as well be a boat —
'I can't climb into it. I'm too old.'

*

'Age seasons me, gives me zest' —
he recites, tapping rhythm
on the fretwork of his own chest.

*

'The struggle is against words' —
the poet fulfilled, poured out.

*

'Should I say it again
to get the mistake out?'

*

When you travel by boat you stay
longer, wherever you're destined.

*

A beautiful soul in search of a roof;
from the white margin, your mother's
'All we can do is root for you.'

*

The uncrossable river,
crossed forever.

Bridie Hinchey's

Now that we have dismantled the last of Bridie's house,
turned her water off at the road, reduced her scantlings
and purlins to kindling for our own stove, and wrapped
her aerial cable around her aerial pole, our children ask
for the story of their mother going as a girl to Bridie's

only to be told, 'Five minutes sooner and you'd have caught
me doing The Dying Swan', which we are left, heating
our house with the last of hers, in Bridie's wake, imagining —
that thronged dark, house lights blazing, Bridie crumpled
on the hearth, wingtips brushing gables, her solitary ecstasy.

Demolishing De Meyboom

I give days moving downwards,
absorbing last sounds, seeing
the view reduce from sky to trees,

singling out beams to bore
and pack with soft explosive,
to become the one on whom

the street door closes definitively.
So much steel and masonry
is being conceived of already

as a Facebook page.
Terminals connect where I am.
A dust cloud blossoms where I have been.

A Plum Tree

for Fiona

When the tree falls, how can the shadow stand?
        — Mary Lavin, '*In the Middle of the Fields*'

We planted two we meant to mean ourselves,
turned so that the longest branch of each
appeared to be reaching towards the other
at the end of the garden, across grass and air.

In their second season, when one's limbs bowed
with young fruit and wasps swarmed to feast,
specks appeared on the tips of the other's leaves
and the white flesh beneath the bark turned brown.

We forgot if the lost one had been me or you
and spoke of replacing it but didn't.
Grass filled in the bare patch. Desiccated roots

and the thin trunk went up like tinder.
A loppers evened off the reaching branch.
The one that prospered came to mean the two.

Automatic Telecom Exchange, Templetuohy

It is as dark in there as inside a head.
This is where Jimmy Carey's forge stood.

When he lays his hand to the bellows
the whole switchboard lights up.

St Constant, Maurs

It was full night and the hay
frenzy was on. I lay in
the turned sward to catch

my breath and look
at the lone pear tree
on the hill with the moon

behind it, like a tree
in a stage set, and drifted off.
Then the great baler,

and a hare in the sward
next to mine started and took
off and woke me. The two

of us had been sound
to the world. To the woman
of the old house's

'*Bonne Nuet*',
I replied '*Bonne Nuit*',
hardly able to speak

for 'night' being feminine.
How could I have known
I would never love the Earth

as intensely again?
I'd been lying there
trying to figure out

the difference
between the sounds
for '*pear*' and '*sin*'

before giving in
to sleep. I might be lying
in that same hay yet.

A Christening

Come, Eurycleia, move the great bed outside the bedroom that he himself built and make it up with fleeces and blankets and brightly coloured rugs.
                    — *The Odyssey*, Book 23

The night he left I left the night light
on all night, and took the stool we used
to climb up into the high bed up with me,
remembering the night we christened the bed —

his head whacking off the headboard,
me moist as a slipway, hard welts nested
in the softness on his palms hard against me,
the stink of resin rising off him, the taste

of it on the fingers he slipped into my mouth,
our wedding linen sticky with it, green leaves
everywhere and autumn weeks away,
warm draughts of night heat wafting up

between the struts, him whispering how
he loved my big belly like a full sail,
the thwack of stiff cloth against the mast,
the print of bed timbers through the mattress

on my back when we tacked and he steered
me round. And I remember the haft of an old oar
he sawed in half to wedge the makeshift bed
against the gable, it slipping free and the bed

feeling as if it was stealing off into the night.
Holding him inside me, afraid to breathe,
I knew the one thing anchoring us then
was the one free arm I'd wound around

the branches. And I could think of no good
reason why I should hold on. So,
when he had me where he wanted me
and I had him, I told him to batten down his hatches.

And I let go.

The Five Trees, November 14th

Though it leaves in its wake a trail of splintered wood,
the hedge cutter touches, on their heads, not the least bud.

First Frost

for Grace

All I see is her bare feet on the deal stairs, her face,
when she sees the world turned white, turn towards
our two faces to ask, 'What did you do?' — as if we
might be able somehow to account for all that beauty.

A Cauldron in Dunshaughlin

i.m. Michael Kenny (1926-2013)

At rest with its mouth,
because it looked
so like an upturned bell
bolted to the ground

in Dunshaughlin,
I struck that famine cauldron
with my bare hand,
and it is ringing still.

A Water Trough in County Monaghan

for Pat Kennan

1

The iron clapper has sunk to the bottom
of an upturned bell horses are drinking from.

2

The fleshy clappers of their tongues toll
rainwater when they quench their thirsts.

3

When the bell's struck, its fresh note ripples.
Striking the wrong note is unimaginable.

The Five Trees, December 17th

Kept exactly as they were left, untouched,
their made beds are eiderdowned with frost.

Local History

His password is the townland he was born in,
the townland her people hail from;
hers is the surname of the only man
she ever slept with, with whom she will be buried.

Together, before the Local History PC,
they google the *Ordnance Survey of Ireland*,
select their parish from a drop menu
and head down a road they know the potholes in.

Bog appears as a blank screen,
yet she has a name in her head
for a part of it not on the map;
Ballinavaddog, Gáilte, Drumsawry,

Summerbank, Staholmog, Hesty.
He pans, and zooms, and steers the mouse.
Hesty. From the passenger seat
she prompts him where to go.

The Names of the Fields

I THE SMOOTHERN IRON, RATOATH

She lifts it to her cheek to test
its heat, and works creases out
while the other iron heats.

He turns the team with a click
of his tongue; the coulter hisses,
cooled by clay as it leaves its crease.

2 CROOKED TREE FIELD, CONNELLSTOWN

As she watches him slip into the woods,
his hands overflowing with axe-heads,
like an apple harvester's with windfalls,

to search for branches to make axe-handles,
she calls after him, 'There's nothing straight
in this world, Alfie, not even in those woods.'

3 NEWTOWN, KILMAINHAMWOOD

She can walk them in her mind
and in her mind say the names
like a prayer, but draws the line

at the pain of having to look
at the glass gone from the panes,
the chimney stacks like cenotaphs.

At the River

a postscript

I feel them again
when I reach
for change to pay
to cross the river —

the crocus bulbs,
wrapped in muslin,
they passed out
in the atrium —

and place one
in the palm of the woman
who reaches
from the booth.

Then a pause
happens.
The barrier lifts.
And I pass on.

A Knapsack

As if one didn't hear or the other hasn't spoken,
when he lays a likeness of John Scotus down
for a sturdy knapsack to carry all he needs
and intimates, 'You'll take four-fifty . . .',

he is his father's son, as is the saddler Melady
who registers the accent, the tendered note,
and, saying nothing, sets a strange heptagon
bearing a woodcock plummeting between them.

So philosophy and nature must be exchanged
and the common ground found before the poet,
weighed down and lightened, turns from the town
to take up his path again, which is the river's path.

At Gaffney

This morning spent with Tommy and Mary Christie
is how I would like Eternity to be.
Two sods in the grate will be keeping the fire lit
as fresh tea draws on its stand at the grate
and the talk turns from cricket pads and bats
to the banshee and vixen being one and the same.
If Jim Curley drops in he'll describe molten lead
being poured into an egg shell half bedded in sand
to make the perfect weight for catching eels,
which leads to talk of eel skins as strops for razors,
then a game of remembering all the brand names
of the old blades, until it dawns on someone
that we might wander out to stretch our legs
and check on the day, and be amazed at the raspberry canes.

Autumn, 1977

I am a vault.
Not a word said here
goes outside these four walls.

There is still light out,
but growing cold, and he has
gone too far, for him, this time.

In full uniform, he has taken it
into his head to take, in the sixth
month of her pregnancy, the sweeping

brush to her. And she, on her knees,
is sheltering from the blows
under the table we eat from.

The only ones the boy who sees
can tell, as he stands with his back
to the one wall with no door in it,

is him or her, and he
is miles away by now, riding
shotgun in a squad car, taking

names, checking *bona fides*,
keeping an eye on late houses,
houses of ill repute where callers

come and go at all hours, as she,
needing a doctor or a priest,
is getting to her feet.

They have come to this.
There is no need to speak,
and the girls are due from school.

Her tear-streaked face up close
to mine, streaked from crying,
is saying, 'Everything is fine.

Everything is fine.' If it stops
here, she will be getting away
light. I will not breathe

a word to a soul.
I will keep mum.
I will be the death of him.

A Swinging Brick

What did I know of the heart, or think I knew,
repeating to her what a friend told me
to remember, that the heart — oblong, resilient, little
muscle — is a pump and not a filter, as if that
was a thing she didn't know. It is too late now
to have kept silence. I think of her, 'It's well
for them that has one and not a swinging brick',

how that silenced me because it spoke
of a life before this life, and a life before that
again, when she was a slim girl bringing
bread and sweet tea to a man wielding a scythe
who paused to take in all he had done,
all he has to do before the rain comes on
and the light fails and, hand in hand, they go.

Notes

page 14   '*cló*': print, type

page 20   Negus: commonly port mixed with hot water, spiced and sugared. In Charles Finch's *A Death in the Small Hours* it settles the stomach wonderfully.

page 28   'Midnichestown, Midnicht's town, Midnightstown, Midnithstown, Midnycht's town, Midnythestoun, Midnytheston, Mindnichiston, Ministown, Minnichtestoun, Mynissetoun, Mynnisetoun, Mynnyghteston, Mynnynestoun, Mynnyngeston, Mynyghteston.' *Calendar of the Gormanston Register from the original in the possession of the Right Honourable The Viscount of Gormanston* (Royal Society of Antiquaries of Ireland, 1916).

page 37   *Arles* (or Arless, historically Ardlisse, from the Irish *Ard Lios*). The similarities between the southern French town and the southern Laois village, close to the Carlow border, end with the name.

page 44   *Brú síos mé:* 'Push me back down' (into the lifeboat).

page 50   A native of Gurtmullen, Roscrea, County Tipperary, a private in the Irish Guards and a lifelong non-smoker, Fred Bennett died of TB in 1920. His brass cigarette box and its intact contents were auctioned in September 2012.

page 58   The airman was Horst Febber, Paumern No. 73712/49.

page 82   This poem commemorates a purchase made on Trimgate Street in Navan in the summer of 1979 by Seamus Heaney during the course of a walk along the Boyne with the *New Yorker* writer Anthony Bailey.

Acknowledgements

Acknowledgements are due to the editors of the following journals and periodicals where some of these poems, or versions of them, were published first: *Atlanta Review, Boyne Berries, Cyphers, The Honest Ulsterman, The Manchester Review, The Meath Chronicle, Íris Éireannach Nua/New Hibernia Review, Poetry Ireland Review, The SHOp* and *The Stinging Fly.*

'The Verge of Tears', '02.07.2012', 'In Memory' and 'At the River' appeared together as an e-chapbook titled *The Night Ahead*, published on 2 July 2013 by Kenneth Keating's www.smithereenspress.com. A version of 'The Names of the Fields' appeared in *The Field Names of County Meath* (Meath Field Names Project, 2013).

The author gratefully acknowledges a bursary in Literature from An Comhairle Ealaíon/The Arts Council in 2009.

Warmest thanks are due to the Tyrone Guthrie Centre at Annaghmakerrig in Newbliss. Where else would the horses have been drinking from a bell?